THE TRENDMASTER'S GUIDE

The
TRENDMASTER'S
Guide

GET A JUMP ON WHAT
YOUR CUSTOMER WANTS NEXT

Robyn Waters

Illustrated by Lindsay Van De Weghe

Portfolio

PORTFOLIO
Published by the Penguin Group
Penguin Group (USA) Inc., 375 Hudson Street, New York 10014, U.S.A.
Penguin Group (Canada), 10 Alcorn Avenue, Toronto, Ontario, Canada M4V 3B2
(a division of Pearson Penguin Canada Inc.)
Penguin Books Ltd, 80 Strand, London WC2R 0RL, England
Penguin Ireland, 25 St Stephen's Green, Dublin 2, Ireland
(a division of Penguin Books Ltd)
Penguin Books Australia Ltd., 250 Camberwell Road, Camberwell, Victoria 3124, Australia
(a division of Pearson Australia Group Pty Ltd)
Penguin Books India Pvt Ltd, 11 Community Centre, Panchsheel Park, New Delhi – 110 017, India
Penguin Group (NZ), Cnr Airborne and Rosedale Roads, Albany, Auckland 1310, New Zealand
(a division of Pearson New Zealand Ltd)
Penguin Books (South Africa) (Pty) Ltd, 24 Sturdee Avenue,
Rosebank, Johannesburg 2196, South Africa

Penguin Books Ltd, Registered Offices: 80 Strand, London WC2R 0RL, England

First published in 2005 by Portfolio,
a member of Penguin Group (USA) Inc.

1   3   5   7   9   10   8   6   4   2

Copyright © RW Trend, LLC, 2005
All rights reserved

Portions of this book appeared in the author's pamphlet, *The Trendmaster's Guide From A–Z.*

Publisher's Note: This publication is designed to provide accurate and authoritative information in regard to the subject matter covered. It is sold with the understanding that the publisher is not engaged in rendering legal, accounting or other professional services. If you require legal advice or other expert assistance, you should seek the services of a competent professional.

LIBRARY OF CONGRESS CATALOGING IN PUBLICATION DATA

Waters, Robyn.
The trendmaster's guide : get a jump on what your customer wants next / Robyn Waters.
p.   cm.
Includes bibliographical references.
ISBN 1-59184-091-0
1. Sales forecasting.   2. Business forecasting.   3. Fads.   4. Design.   I. Title.
HF5415.2.W38   2005
658.8'18—dc22   2004065031

This book is printed on acid-free paper. ∞

Printed in the United States of America
Set in Horley Old Style
Designed by Daniel Lagin

To Helen,
who not only helped me find my voice,
but also encouraged me to use it.

CONTENTS

INTRODUCTION

Welcome to the world of trends.

It's a myth that trends can only be spotted early by überhip Bohemian types who are ever-so-much cooler than everyone else.

Trends are indicators that point to what's going on in the hearts and minds of consumers. And there's a big difference between a trend tracker and what I call a Trendmaster. A trend tracker looks at the signs to help his or her business stay *up to the minute*. A Trendmaster, however, uses the trend information to determine *where that minute is going*. Trendmasters start out by observing a trend, but then they translate that trend information into a direction that makes sense for their companies and their customers.

My goal for *The Trendmaster's Guide* is to simplify and demystify the art and science of trend. In it I share my favorite tips, examples, and tricks of the trade. Every letter from A to Z offers an insight into how to navigate the unknown and a practical tip to help you prepare for what's next.

So, Robyn, did you major in Trend Studies at the Sorbonne, Harvard, or Stanford?

I have spent the last thirty years studying trends and their impact on businesses—a calling that I discovered completely by accident. And take it from a girl from rural Minnesota: you don't need an Ivy League diploma, an MBA, or an all-black wardrobe to become a Trendmaster.

I used to ride my horse to one of the last one-room country schoolhouses in the state. My graduating class from Rockford High was fifty-two students, the largest ever. I went on to Mankato State University. When status-obsessed people ask me "And where did you go to college?" I politely answer "Mankato State." They usually just look at me blankly. If they bother to ask where in the world Mankato is, I tell them it was where Pa Ingalls (from *Little House on the Prairie*) went when he hitched up the wagons to go into the big city for supplies.

I got my first job at Donaldson's Department Stores as an assistant fashion coordinator, during one of the worst job markets since the Depression. For a young woman fresh out of college, this was considered a fairly glamorous (though notoriously low-paying) job. As assistant fashion coordinator I produced Butte Knit and Leslie Fay fashion shows, and one year even the St. Paul Winter Carnival Queen of the Snows Fashion Show. I styled fashion photography ads and catalogs on location. The Haggar leisure suit ads were particularly fun—the male models were so handsome! I also worked closely with buyers, advising them on what to buy now to put on the selling floor a year down the road.

At the ripe old age of twenty-four I headed south for a much bigger job. I became the Director of Fashion, Special Events, and Public Relations for McRae's, a family-owned, carriage-trade department store in Jackson, Mississippi. McRae's was progressive in a lot of ways, but not when it came to women in management. Let's face it—I was a Yankee, I walked too fast, I talked too fast, and I wouldn't get coffee for the guys. I was an anomaly. But I loved the business, and I was excited by the adventure of life in retail.

In my role as public relations director I was a frequent guest on *Mississippi Morning Live* (a local TV show) to talk about upcoming events at the store. It was interesting to appear with a story about a Lord Wedgwood event for fine china and be sandwiched in between a piece on catfish farming and a segment on how to make fried pickles.

In the mideighties I moved to Boston as a men's fashion director for Jordan Marsh Department Stores. High style and high fashion were all the rage, damn the cost. It was the "greed is good" era and Jordan Marsh was one of the high-class department stores of the day. I found myself sitting in the front row at designer fashion shows, rubbing shoulders with fashion icons like Gianfranco Ferre and Giorgio Armani, and having dinner at the Missoni's villa outside of Milan. At that time, trends were nearly always set by the top fashion designers—from the top down to the street, so to speak.

I was still producing fashion shows, only now they were black-tie events staged for *GQ* magazine. One year we featured a Harley-Davidson motorcycle for the bridal finale. The bride went down the aisle sidesaddle on the back of the hog, veil flying, with the groom looking gritty and gorgeous as he vroomed down the runway. All this to the soundtrack of Sonny and Cher singing "I've Got You Babe."

It was also my first experience with private label and product development. Stores began to realize that they could effectively offer exclusive designs under their own brand names and give the customer a better value than many of the well-known national brands did. As men's fashion director I selected stripes for men's boxer shorts, colors for cashmere mufflers, and swatches for expensive suitings. Best of all, I got to style the men's silk foulard ties—a great excuse to spend a few weeks every summer in Lake Como, Italy.

Eventually, all the greed, glamour, and excess of the eighties caught up with the economy. Men who had been buying high-end designer fashions decided that they didn't really need $1,000 tuxedo shirts or $100 dress shirts. The designer business stumbled, and many high-end department stores went the way of the dinosaur.

In November 1992, a group of us huddled around a speakerphone were told that Jordan Marsh as we knew it would cease to exist. It was being merged into Abraham & Strauss, based in Brooklyn, New York. We had the option to compete for our jobs with our counterparts at A&S, but we'd have to be willing to move to Brooklyn. Thoroughly depressed and in shock, I drove home through the first snowstorm of the season with the realization that I no longer had a job. It was an abrupt halt to the glamour era, to say the least.

Expect More. Pay Less.

After stewing, worrying, and crying through most of the weekend, I went into the office on Monday morning. We'd all been asked to stay through the transition, so at least I still had an office to go to. I was amazed to find thirty-four voice-mail messages! I had condolences, job offers, interview opportunities, and words of encouragement from the many vendors and manufacturers with whom I'd worked over the years.

I flew all over the country, interviewing, trying to imagine myself doing something different. Although I was a department store snob at the time, I sensed that things were beginning to change. There was a value shift going on, and the emerging trend was that most Americans were no longer going to be dictated to by designers on high. Trends were beginning to be driven from the street up, not just from the elite fashion designers down.

So when Target invited me to interview for a position in their Trend Department, I was ready to listen. It was Mother's Day weekend and it seemed like a good excuse to go home to Minneapolis (where Target is based). I was thoroughly impressed with Target, and I took a job there as trend manager for Ready-to-Wear and Children's. I was part of a five-person team of trend managers who worked side by side with the buyers to merchandise and develop products.

We traveled to Europe and Asia on a regular basis, as well as to all the trendy hot spots in the United States. We scouted new retail concepts, shopped for design ideas, went to events like the X-games to get closer to our customers, and worked together with key manufacturers to develop next year's product.

It was a new way to approach trend tracking, and the exact opposite of "runway research." We started with the customers. We tried to get close to their lives, understand their lifestyles, and then take the fashion trends that we saw happening (on the street, in the stores, at the designer level) and translate them into fashionable, affordable products for Target.

One of the best perks of the job was traveling to Saint-Tropez every summer to shop the stores and take photos of all the fashionistas disembarking from their yachts. At the time, that was where everyone went to scout the trends for the next summer season. It was a gold mine for bathing suit manufacturers, shoe designers, T-shirt mavens, and children's wear designers.

But I soon realized that all the retailers, designers, and manufacturers were going to the same places, doing the same things, seeing the same trends, and buying the same samples. Was it just coincidence that around that time we began to hear retail analysts, media pundits, and consumers complaining that everything looked alike?

Target was just beginning to evolve from a small, regional discount chain to a national, $48 billion, upscale discounter. Our management had figured out that differentiation was the name of the game if we wanted to grow and prosper. We were painfully aware that we couldn't beat Wal-Mart on price, but we knew that if we could offer our guests (that's what we called our customers) the same well-styled designs that were being sold in the Gap and Banana Republic, Pottery Barn and Crate & Barrel, but at much better prices, then we'd have a reason to exist in the marketplace.

Management laid out a clear vision as to how we were going to make that happen. We were going to be "trend right," customer focused, and design driven. We were going to help make chic cheap, design democratic, and put some real pizzazz into the world of discounting.

I was promoted to trend director and then to vice president of Trend Merchandising. My department grew quickly from eight people to more than one hundred by the end of the nineties. Renamed the Trend and

Design Department, we added more and more design-ers: clothing designers, technical designers, print and pattern designers, even industrial designers.

We had become a full-fledged product-development office, and our cool new stuff helped turn Target into *Tarzhay.* Designers like Michael Graves, Philippe Starck, Mossimo, and Todd Oldham lent credibility to our design philosophy. Our brand promise ("Expect More. Pay Less.") helped make the red bull's-eye as recognizable as the Nike Swoosh or the McDonald's Golden Arches.

In 2002, after ten and a half years with the "bull's-eye brigade," I decided to strike out on my own. Today I work with many different companies as an Ambassador of Trend, a Champion of Design, a Builder of Brands, and a Cheerleader of Possibilities.

You can do it too.

I believe that anyone can use the tools in *The Trendmaster's Guide* to become more aware of the world around them. Even if you weren't born with a trendspotting bone in your body, you don't have to be a follower for-ever. These days no one can afford to be just catching on as others are already moving on! Recognizing and reacting to trends is a *learned skill,* and it can be acquired without extensive time spent in the streets of Milan or the high schools of Orange County.

If you've ever witnessed a trend unfolding and said to yourself, "I should have seen *this* coming," there's hope. You too can become a Trendmaster and get a jump on your competition.

Welcome to a new way of looking at the world!

THE TRENDMASTER'S GUIDE

Is for

ANTENNAE

So . . . you want to spot the next big thing? Chances are you've already seen it. What you need to do is let yourself *recognize it.* Put your antennae out, your periscope up, your scanner on high, and tune in to the little things, the trivial nuances, and the irrelevant data that everyone else misses. On its own, each tidbit is meaningless; strung together, they are *aha*s waiting to be noticed.

Monica Nassif is the creator and founder of Caldrea, a line of all-natural aromatherapeutic cleaning products. She had her antennae out in the early nineties as she watched aromatherapy go from new age to mainstream in the course of a few years.

Spas were the first to feature the healing properties of aromatherapy, using ancient homeopathic recipes to calm, invigorate, rejuvenate, and relax. The cosmetic industry was next, with lines like Origins and Aveda touting the healing properties of the same scents for over-the-counter beauty creams, hand lotions, and bath and hair products.

Then came scented candles in decorative containers. Brands such as Diptyque, Rigaud, and Crabtree and Evelyn featured aromatherapy as a key selling point to their upscale products.

Monica had the idea to incorporate the same properties that American women had come to enjoy in all of these everyday products into upscale cleaning products. She paid attention to what her antennae were picking up and asked questions like "Why couldn't washing your dishes become a pleasurable act of self-healing?" "When did we begin to believe that things had to smell antiseptic to be considered really clean?" and "Why not incorporate bestselling scents like lavender, green tea, and patchouli into dishwashing liquid?"

She hired a chemist and began to experiment, using only the best all-natural ingredients for her products in much the same way that Horst Rechelbacher did in his Aveda spa products. She developed a line consisting of dishwashing liquid, hand soap, and hand lotion and packaged them together in an upscale manner. She devised a handsome caddy to hold the products, and it quickly became a bestselling hostess gift.

Clearly, a $12 bottle of dishwashing detergent needed a unique marketing strategy; traditional grocery stores weren't interested in carrying Monica's products in the cleaning aisle, next to the Dawn and Joy that retailed for $1 a bottle. Knowing that she could never go head-to-head with the giant brands, she began selling Caldrea to upscale boutiques and gift stores. She worked with the owners and managers to ensure an appropriate presentation that highlighted the unique properties of her products.

Today, Caldrea is a full-scale line of home-cleaning products that includes laundry soap, ironing water, and even nostalgic cleaning tools. Monica has also written a book called *Spring Cleaning: The Spirit of Keeping Home,* describing how she sees housework as a simple way to have a sense of control in our not-so-simple world.

People tend to file away what doesn't immediately make sense. That's exactly the stuff we should be paying attention to! To cultivate awareness, contemplate meditation. When you learn to empty your mind, you'll be surprised how much room is in there. Once you've let down your barriers, your antennal frequency can be dialed high, your trend reception magnified, and your instinct and intuition maximized.

Is for

BIG PICTURE

The deluge of trend options available today can be confusing. Combine this overwhelming input with type-A personalities who obsess over details, and you have a bad retail recipe: over-designed products that spring from over-conceived strategies. We can't see the proverbial forest for the trees. Big Pictures can be hard to frame, but they're worth looking for. Big Picture = Big Opportunity.

Dutch Boy painted a different perspective with their signature line of paints when they began to look at painting through the eyes of their customers.

Most major paint companies at the time were spending millions of dollars on research and development, working to develop a better paint product. The goal was to find paints that were shinier and brighter, lasted longer, cleaned better, or were less toxic. Scientists tweaked ingredients and tinkered with manufacturing processes in an effort to find a better formula.

Yet no one ever stopped to ask why paint still came in those heavy cans with lids that were messy and hard to pry off, and handles that were uncomfortable to use. No one asked why there wasn't a spout to control the paint as it poured out into the roller pan. And why the cleanup had to be so messy and why the lid invariably had paint gunked up on it and, when dry, became very hard to open up again.

It took a designer with a different perspective to ask the unasked questions. Some clever soul figured that maybe it wasn't a better *paint* that was desired. Maybe it was a better *painting experience.*

By simply redesigning the paint can into a lightweight plastic jug with a handle, screw cap, and pour spout, Dutch Boy trounced the competition before the paint dried. Sales increased by double-digit increments, and they won prestigious design awards for their new paint "can."

Finding the big picture has everything to do with perspective. When you're lost in the forest, step back—*way* back—and reexamine your original principles. Ask yourself if you're asking the right questions. Test your assumptions from every angle. The most important thing is to look at the problem through the eyes and lives of the end consumer.

Is for

CONNECT THE DOTS

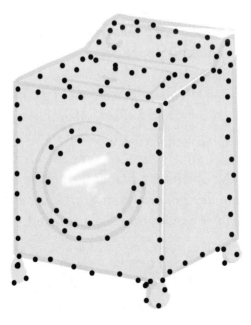

An interesting fact catches your attention. A related tidbit pops up out of nowhere. A random comment reinforces a budding thought. Hey . . . pay attention! Your trend dots are begging to be connected. Taken individually, each "dot" may not mean a lot. Connected, a pattern emerges that often points to a developing trend—in time to do something about it.

Not long ago the laundry room was one of the most functional, boring, hidden, off-limits-to-company rooms in the home. It certainly wasn't a room that you showed off to your guests or bragged about to your neighbors. No shelter magazines featured articles about Luxury Laundry Room Makeovers. Gourmet kitchens, yes. Spa bathrooms, of course. Luxury laundry rooms . . . unheard of.

Not the case if you knew how to connect the dots!

Martha Stewart brought a new dignity and level of accomplishment to simple tasks like cleaning windows, doing laundry, and organizing pantries. Her magazine, *Martha Stewart Living,* gentrified the art of housekeeping and turned housecleaning into homemaking.

At the same time, manufacturers of cleaning products were busy reframing the world of housecleaning. *Business 2.0* featured an article titled "Selling Cool in a Bottle—of Dish Soap. How a startup called Method roused a tired category and turned household cleaning products into objects of desire." Cleaning products as objects of desire? Wasn't that a stretch?

Not really. Ten million dollars in sales later, Method's eye-catching design, fresh natural ingredients, and trendy, modern, natural scents made customers want to show off this dish detergent as an object of desire. Women love to store the sleek designer bottle *next* to the sink instead of *under* it to showcase this cleaning wonder.

Around the same time, Restoration Hardware expanded their laundry and cleaning section to feature extensive presentations of Good Home luxury cleaning products. They were looking for a way to take some of the pain out of the cleaning process and inject a little pleasure. Christine Dimmick, the founder of Good Home products, envisioned a company that would allow her to re-create a way of life reminiscent of growing up on a Texas farm with her grandparents. Good Home packages their lavender liquid fabric softener in old-fashioned, stopper-type glass bottles.

Spotting any dots yet?

It used to be that a washer and dryer were functional white boxes that cleaned your clothes. Period. The average retail price for a new pair was around $800. Then Whirlpool worked their design magic on the humble household tool and introduced the Duet—a high-end pair of ultraperformance-oriented, beautifully designed, sleek machines that some homeowners dubbed "the Ferrari of washing machines." At $2,000 a pair, no one initially thought they'd sell that well. However, within just a few years, Whirlpool had captured over 20 percent of the American market with their luxury product.

Maytag responded with the Neptune Drying Center—a dryer with a top cabinet specifically designed for clothes you'd never dream of putting in a regular dryer. The Neptune dries clothes three times faster, removes odors, and minimizes wrinkles through a unique combination of clever design, steam application, temperature control, and airflow management. Whew! That's a lot of engineering for what used to be a clothesline.

Owners of "McMansions" around the country scooped up these design wonders as the new luxury status product. Most didn't want to hide $2,000 worth of high-end equipment in a basement. Interior designers connected the dots and responded with new designs that deliberately integrated the laundry room into the home's living quarters and design schemes. Think granite countertops to fold laundry on. Think multiple laundry rooms, one on each floor, to minimize basket schlepping. Think fine, custom-built cabinetry with special sorting compartments for dirty laundry and shelving for all those luxury cleaning products. And while you're at it, how about a plasma screen TV?

Homebuilders that connected the dots realized early on the importance of the new luxury laundry rooms. They discovered that "if you build it, they will come." The women came. The houses sold.

Take notice of small details that catch your attention, even if at the time they don't seem to make any sense. It's usually an indication that the right side of your brain is engaged and mulling things over. It's only a matter of time before the dots connect and *Eureka!* occurs.

Is for

DESIGN

Once you've identified a trend that you want to develop, how do you go from concept to reality? Design is the tool used to translate an idea into an actual product. Currently, we're in the midst of a design revolution. Professor Robert Hayes of the Harvard Business School launched one of the first salvos of the revolution when he said, "Fifteen years ago companies competed on price. Today it's quality. Tomorrow, it's design." No doubt about it, tomorrow has arrived.

Steve Jobs, cofounder of Apple, was one of the pioneers of the design revolution.

When the iMac computer was unveiled it caused a sensation with its sleek, groundbreaking design. When Jobs hired Jonathon Ives to design the new iMac, he told Ives *not* to think about a computer as a machine, but rather as a creative tool, an extension of the person using it. The result was a user-friendly, organic, colorful design that eliminated the need for a clumsy hard drive underneath the desk.

The runaway success of the iPod is another salvo in the race to use good design to drive sales and profit. The iPod quickly became a status symbol as well as the fashion accessory of the moment. The sleek, all-white design of the original iPod was cleverly highlighted in the award-winning advertising campaign that featured silhouettes of different customers enjoying their music, their way.

Today, the telltale white bud earphones denote that you are one of the "enlightened." When the new Mini iPod was launched it caused an even greater sensation at retail. "Poddicts" raced to be the first on the block to own one in their choice of fashion-forward metallic colors.

Not only was the physical design of the iPod revolutionary, it also reframed how we listen to, buy, and play music. The idea that you could go online any time of the day or night to purchase only the songs you want, and then combine them into your own personalized playlists, won the hearts of even non–Apple lovers.

It's important to realize that good design is about more than function and aesthetics. Good design can infuse

your products with soul as well as deliver beauty to the bottom line. The future belongs to those with the creative skills to do just that. Hire and nurture great design talent . . . it's your best offense.

Is for

EDIT

Here's a lesson I've learned over the years: too much information without editing is toxic. It's necessary to identify and focus on what's really important and edit out any distractions. Too many options or choices can be confusing, which can turn your customers away.

We live in a complicated world with an overabundance of options. Seth Godin, in *Fast Company* magazine, recently suggested that Americans are currently dealing with a "scarcity shortage." A scarcity of shortages? That sounds like an oxymoron, doesn't it?

But think about it. We tend to think that in America it's abundance that keeps the economy going strong. Seth points out that perhaps we are victims of too many things flooding the marketplace. Maybe that's why everything ends up looking alike. When that happens, everything becomes a little less valuable, and a lot less special.

J. Walker Smith, president of Yankelovich Partners,

stated at a CPG summit in 2004 that consumers are beginning to feel a "claustrophobia of abundance," and that they may now prefer fewer options from which to make choices. It seems that there may be a point where choice tyrannizes people more than it liberates them.

One interesting result of this overabundance of choice is the rise of a new breed of store where the selection of product is limited strictly to the discriminating taste of the buyer or boutique owner. They shop the market across various categories and pre-edit the assortment. Instead of offering every style and brand of running shoe, for instance, they may choose what they feel is the best style from Nike, one from D&G, and perhaps a third from Prada. Thus the customer only has to choose from among three styles, not the thirty or forty that would be featured in a traditional shoe store. Collette's in Paris, Corso Como in Milan, and Microzine in London are examples of this new, pre-edited retail concept.

Ban laundry lists! Focus on what's really important, special, or remarkable. Force yourself and your team to edit to a *top ten list*, or even better, the *three big ideas*, or more perfectly, the *one really important thing* that will make a difference to your customer. Edit, focus, *maximize!*

Is for

FUSION

Trends with real staying power are often a series of smaller trends fused together. Trends that intersect and complement each other are more likely to be embraced by the consumer. When fusion occurs, it's much easier to offer a product that is in sync with your customers' values.

Gogurt is a yogurt snack served in a squeeze tube. It fuses the trends of convenience, portability, and healthy snack alternatives into a unique and saleable concept. When General Mills and Yoplait first introduced Gogurt into the marketplace, they knew that by making it *fun* for kids and *easy* for Mom they would be able to capitalize on this fusion.

Gogurt offered a unique and powerful marketing opportunity because it addressed needs as well as desires. The success of Gogurt not only revolutionized the yogurt category, it created an entirely new marketing concept across the snack-food industry. Today you can find everything from peanut butter to applesauce to pudding in squeeze tubes for kids on the go.

Think of each small trend you observe as a thread that you can weave, twist, plait, braid, knit, or splice together with other common strands into a tapestry of opportunity. Get creative. Create a masterpiece.

G

Is for

GRACE AND GUTS

Trend leadership, like other forms of leadership, often requires a measure of grace and guts to succeed. In order to be launched effectively into mainstream consciousness, a new trend needs to take a leap of faith and courageously reframe the landscape. It takes guts to be first, to be different. If researched well, understood properly, and translated gracefully, a new trend can be adopted and endorsed in a startlingly short amount of time.

It took guts for Frank Gehry to propose his futuristic, brave new design for the Guggenheim Museum in Bilbao. It took guts for the town fathers to take the leap to approve the innovative design for their city. Many people in the art world thought this venture was sheer folly. Bilbao was a decaying town on a polluted river in what was then considered the Rust Belt of Spain. No one, they thought, would venture that far out of the way to go to a museum.

From the moment the building was completed, it was

clear that that would not be the case. The building was so magnificent that it created a major stir around the world. The titanium panels that sheath the exterior change color with the movement of the sun and the clouds. The building actually seems to undulate like a giant fish on the river. The elegant lines of the enormous structure sit in close proximity to a waterfront that has come alive with pedestrian walkways and an outdoor sculpture garden that is enjoyed by thousands of visitors each year.

Since its completion, this gutsy, graceful edifice has completely revitalized the entire downtown shopping area of Bilbao as well. The once sleepy city center has been reinvigorated with outdoor cafés, elegant shopping boutiques, fine restaurants, and new hotels. The economy is robust, and the exhibitions continue to draw visitors from around the world.

Grace never goes out of style. When you're tempted to do something that flies in the face of good taste, don't. My advice is to err on the side of elegance, refinement, and class. Yes, there's a lot of bad taste out there that sells just fine, but is that what you want to be known for? It takes courage to stand for your convictions, but if you ignore this advice you may find yourself in a free-fall, with a very hard landing.

H

Is for

HEAD, HANDBAG, AND HEART

This is also known as my "3H Design Theory." When new designers were hired at Target, I wanted to make sure they understood the importance of being customer focused. The 3H Theory highlights the three main reasons a customer buys something. The *head* is about need: "I'm out of toothpaste, time to buy." The *handbag* is about value and price: "It's on sale, so I'd better stock up." The *heart* is about desire: "I *love* that and I have to have it."

When Target embarked on the Starck Reality Design Project with world-famous designer Philippe Starck, none of us really knew what to expect. As the head of a design department, I knew we'd learn a lot about the technical world of design, but I had no idea we'd learn so much about the heart.

One of the first products Philippe proposed was a sippy cup, one of those sturdy, unspillable cups with a lid that kids can drink from without fear of messing up the kitchen table or spilling onto Mommy's new sofa. Most mothers would consider sippy cups a standard piece of child-rearing equipment—a need.

The design that Starck proposed was unique, to say the least. It resembled a clear, cut-crystal, double-handled loving cup on a pedestal. Initially the buyers were hesitant to even consider the design. It looked so impractical on the pedestal, as though it were *more* likely to spill, not *less*.

To convince the buyers to go forward with the counterintuitive design, Starck first demonstrated that if the vessel did tip or was knocked over, the liquid wouldn't spill. Therefore the *head* was satisfied; the product was useful and it worked. Because we were Target, the design, although chic, could still be made inexpensively and retail for $3.49—still a value for the *handbag* test.

It was Philippe's passionate belief that every little girl should feel like a princess when she drank from the sippy cup, just as Mommy and Daddy feel when they sipped champagne from fine cut crystal. Ultimately he convinced the merchants to think with their *hearts* about this merchandising decision. The sippy cup was displayed on the aisle endcaps, was featured in fashion editorials around the country, and became an icon for the entire Starck Reality Design Project.

Connecting to the hearts of your customers will help you deliver products with WOW! This is not a new idea. Aristotle said: "You don't persuade people through intellect—you do it through emotion."

Is for

INSTINCT AND INTUITION

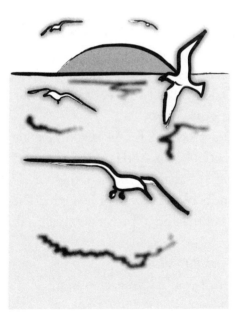

The corporate world today is in love with *six sigma* and other statistical, quantitative methods for judging quality. Facts and figures are important and shouldn't be ignored, of course, but they aren't the whole story.

I have a few out-of-print books that I really treasure, and one is a small book by Bennett Goodspeed called *The Tao Jones Averages: A Guide to WholeBrained Investing*. It's dedicated to "everyone who has the guts to follow their guts."

It was the product of a Madison Avenue think tank firm, Inferential Focus, and is loosely based on Lao Tsu's *Tao te Ching*, the ancient "Book of the Way," which is basically a handbook of Eastern philosophy. There are many translations of the Tao. One version begins this way:

> *Open yourself to the Tao,*
> *   then trust your natural responses:*
> *   and everything will fall into place.*

This is great trend advice. (Actually, I think Lao Tsu may have been the first Trendmaster, and if so I am honored to follow in his footsteps.)

The Tao Jones Averages taught me the meaning of the word *analexia*. Analexia is described as a "societal disease," and refers to the conviction that if something can't be analyzed or measured, it isn't real. (Bean counters are particularly prone to this disease.)

When legions of number crunchers descend on an organization, they look for ways to measure *everything* about *everything*. When that happens, I think much of the creative process is at risk. I'm not saying that numbers, analyses, and best processes aren't important. But there's another side of the brain that needs to be heard.

Keep in mind that all analyses measure results only *after* something has already happened. Trend tracking speculates about what *might* happen based on things that are *constantly changing*. Following your intuition and listening to your instincts have been all but forgotten in today's corporate environment. If it weren't for visionaries who knew how to *go with their instincts*, we'd be living in a world without Post-it notes, FedEx, and Starbucks double tall skim lattes.

Lao Tsu recommends in the *Tao te Ching* that we "discard knowledge and the people would benefit a hundredfold." He also suggests of man that "even though he may be a 'walking encyclopedia' he is really a misguided fool." There are more than a few "misguided fools" walking the corporate halls these days. I think it's time to start a "right-brain" revolution.

Einstein was a pretty smart guy. He believed that "not everything that can be counted counts, and not everything that counts can be counted." Remember that the next time you are plowing through piles of data and feel out of touch with your gut.

Is for

JUST FOR ME

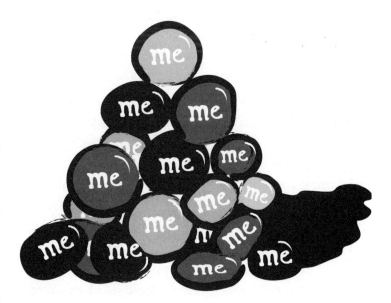

Trend tracking used to be a way to cater to the masses. By its implicit definition, a trend was something that everyone wanted. Well, things have changed. Trend for the sake of trend is not very trendy! The new mantra is "just for me." Customization is the name of the game. Self-expression is key.

Henry Ford introduced our modern industrial world to the cost and time savings of mass production. He boasted that his customers could have any color they wanted, as long as it was black. That approach will not get you very far in today's marketplace.

In the Experience Economy, customization allows a product created for the masses to be personalized to the point where each consumer feels it's all about a special experience for them: their needs, their wants, their tastes, their lives. Some of the most successful products and services today are acknowledgments of this major trend shift.

The iPod revolutionized how we get and listen to music. The individual selects the songs she wants to purchase, and combines them into her own personalized playlists. Pundits have referred to the phenomenon as "Me, Myself, and iPod."

TiVo allows you to become your own TV programmer. You watch what you want to watch, when you want to watch it, without commercials if you choose.

Target, the upscale mass discounter, recently launched "Target to a T," an online custom-ordering process for clothing "made to order."

Starbucks offers nineteen thousand different ways to "customize your cup," and in many locations the barista personally knows "the usual" order of the day for many regular customers.

Meanwhile, the car business has done a great job of taking Henry Ford's original idea of mass production and turning it into a process for mass customization.

Ninety-five percent of all Mini Coopers are customized. The company instituted a "Where's My Baby" online program designed to track each custom Mini through the production process to make the eight-to-twelve-week wait a little more interesting. They were somewhat surprised to learn that over half of all customers named their "baby" . . . hence the name of the program. To acknowledge this phenomenon, Mini ran an ad campaign titled "Younique."

In a similar vein, Toyota's new Scion XB is marketed as "a cheap car with audacious accessories for the discriminating body-piercer." It offers eighteen-to thirty-five-year-olds their very own version of mass customization. The boxy "portable boom boxes," as they are affectionately called, can be customized with thirty-eight different options—including the color of their steering wheel, the colors of the LED lights on the dashboard, specially designed cup holders, seat covers, and more.

Even the food business is finding unique ways to cater to the tastes of the individual. Cold Stone Creamery customizes your cone while giving you a unique ordering experience. You select the type of cone you want, your flavor (or flavors) of ice cream, and then your "mix-ins" such as Reeses Pieces, black cherries, and M&Ms. Your treat is customized by blending the ice cream and mix-ins together with metal spatulas on a cold marble slab, hence the name "Cold Stone."

M&Ms now offers customers the ability to go online and customize special assortments by allowing them to select from nineteen unique colors. They'll also print your name or a special greeting on the candies.

And Jones Soda invites customers to upload their own images to be turned into customized labels for their unique-flavored, funky-colored soft drinks.

Don't look for "one size fits all" solutions. Offer options and ideas for customization. Help your customers creatively express their inherent individuality.

Is for

KEEP IT SIMPLE

I don't know what it is about human nature that makes us think that if something is complicated it must be better. Ralph Waldo Emerson was absolutely correct when he observed: "To be simple is to be great. If you keep things simple, the inherent goodness in a good idea will be much easier to find."

Krispy Kreme doughnuts has this concept down to a T. You can't get much more basic than flour, sugar, and yeast. Yet loyal customers will go to extreme lengths to bring home a box of fresh hot Krispy Kreme doughnuts, often waiting in line for hours when a franchise opens in a brand-new territory.

I witnessed this devotion when I vacationed in Hawaii last spring. Hawaiians commute between islands on shuttle flights on a regular basis; they may live on the Big Island, but their jobs may require them to visit the other islands fairly frequently.

When the first Krispy Kreme franchise in Hawaii

opened in Kapalua, Maui, about a mile from the airport, there were the usual long lines of people waiting to buy the hot doughnut delights. *USA Today* reported that this new store was so successful that it was wreaking havoc with the airlines. Commuters were driving through the take-out line at Krispy Kreme on their way to the airport, then bringing boxes of hot doughnuts onboard to share with family and friends when they got home.

Overhead compartments were filled with boxes and boxes of the simple treats, leaving little or no room for regular carry-on baggage. Not only that, the planes smelled like bakeries. To remedy the situation, the airlines were forced to limit the number of boxes each passenger could bring onboard. An official policy was actually drafted to handle the situation. Imagine— all that fuss for a simple ring of pastry.

When in doubt, try a little common sense. Step back and ask if whatever it is you're trying to present could be made simpler, less complicated, more streamlined. Your product or idea will be sure to stand out in a crowd by virtue of its very simplicity.

Is for

LIGHTEN UP

In most cases, tracking trends isn't a matter of life and death. I've seen many people take the whole process way too seriously. I like to remind them that this isn't exactly *brain surgery*. Trying too hard will only complicate things. I discovered throughout my career that the trend trips and product-development meetings that were the most *fun* usually resulted in the best products.

A few years ago the Ready-to-Wear team at Target was sitting in a product-development meeting, struggling to come up with an idea for the perfect T-shirt. We'd just come back from Saint-Tropez with sample bags bulging with trendy new ideas. We wanted to incorporate the right details into this T-shirt to make it fly off the shelves.

Now, a T-shirt shouldn't be that complicated. You merely have to select a fabric, choose an appropriate color palette, and decide if it's going to be long- or short-sleeved, a crew or V-neck. (More or less.)

But we were struggling, literally trying too hard. We decided to take a short break, and when everyone left the room my trend manager went into the sample room and started to rummage around the shelves. She emerged with an armful of hats of all types: cowboy hats, straw beach hats, visors, baseball caps, witch costume hats, and felt berets. She brought them into the room and piled them in the middle of the table.

When everyone came back she asked them each to pick a hat from the pile on the table. Then she asked them to put the hats on their heads. They were not too happy about this (after all, this was serious business) and more than a few rolled their eyes in barely disguised disgust. But a few good souls complied, and eventually everyone was sitting around the conference table looking pretty ridiculous. The manager then asked them to imagine a T-shirt the person who wore such a hat would want. She asked them be imaginative, and started the ball rolling with a clever visualization that included ridiculous features, impossible details, and creative accessories.

By the time we'd gotten halfway around the table we were all laughing and trying to top the last person's idea. At one point, someone said something so ridiculous, so simple, and so perfect that we all stopped and looked at each other in immediate recognition. That was it! It was really very simple. We just needed to check our assumptions at the door and have a little fun with a meeting that had gotten way too serious. The end result was practical yet fun, and a retail success.

When you're stuck in a dark place void of ideas, lighten up! Have some fun. Do something crazy. Deep-six your standard procedures and try operating with a little humor.

Is for

MAGIC BUTTON

A good trend tracker is always on the lookout for what pushes his or her "magic button." Big or small, simple or complicated, a bargain or an extravagance, if it lights *you* up, chances are it will work the same magic for others.

A few years ago I was invited to speak at a conference in Dubai, which is situated along the Persian Gulf, south of Kuwait and east of Saudi Arabia. Unlike most other countries in the region, Dubai does not have vast oil reserves to count on for its continued prosperity. Yet it's an amazing place that really pushed my magic button, and those of many other visitors.

Years ago, a very progressive sheik decided to turn the ancient sailing port into a world-class trading and financial center. He invited the captains of industry and trade to his country and created a modern high-rise city without rival. The port is duty free, and the airport is one of the most modern in the world. He also had the foresight to create a shopping paradise and leisure playland for the wealthy by attracting world-famous golf, tennis, and Formula One racing stars to the region.

As expats from multinational companies flooded into Dubai, space ran short for living quarters. An enterprising developer created a man-made structure off the coast in the Persian Gulf by excavating thousands of tons of boulders from the interior desert and arranging them into the shape of a giant palm tree, called The Palm.

Other than the Great Wall of China, it's the only man-made structure that can be seen from space with the naked eye. Retail shops and entertainment venues have been built along the trunk of the "tree," and luxury homes were placed strategically along the "fronds."

The project was sold out before the development was halfway completed, so the sheik commissioned a second, similar development farther up the coast. Only this time he added a unique touch to the project: on The Palm Jebel there is a poem in Arabic "written" in quarried limestone around the inner ring of the palm fronds. The sheik himself wrote the poem: "Beware the jockey. Not all who ride are knowledgeable."

This project also sold out long before completion, with international celebrities like David Beckham first in line to buy. Just recently, the same developer has announced an even more extravagant project. The World is the third stage in the massive building project. Two hundred and sixty man-made islands in the shape of the countries of the world are being built, with luxury villas and palaces on each island that are reachable only by water. Sir Rod Stewart just purchased "Great Britain" for eighteen million British pounds sterling.

Make it a habit to notice, really notice, what *takes your breath away*, stimulates your senses, ignites your passions, inspires awe, and delivers delight. Keep track, write it down, make a sketch, start a file, but whatever you do, don't lose it.

N

Is for

NO SECRETS

Back in the dark ages, trend trackers were often considered "spies." They wore trench coats, surreptitiously snuck pictures, sketched designs, and shamelessly copied samples. Now, in the age of the Internet, trends spread like viruses. "Word of mouse" is infinitely more powerful than word of mouth. When there are no secrets, information is ubiquitous, and great design has gone democratic, the challenge becomes how to be *unique.*

A few years ago I was getting ready to travel to Hong Kong for Target's product-development meetings with key vendors. I was asked to develop a trend presentation to share with our manufacturing partners. We had just returned from Europe, and I had fresh inspiration in the form of concept samples and photos to share. When I reviewed my proposed presentation with the president of Target, he expressed momentary concern that I may be giving away company secrets by sharing our trend research and direction. Many of the factories and vendors with whom we did business also produced merchandise for our competitors. How could we be sure that they wouldn't share our "secrets" with our competition?

I replied that we couldn't guarantee that the information wouldn't be shared, but that it wouldn't matter because there *were no secrets.* By that, I meant that if pink was the color of the season, all of the trend and design departments for every wholesaler and retailer alike would already know that. After all, we traveled to the same cities, shopped in the same stores, and went at pretty much the same time of year for direction and inspiration. We all subscribed to many of the same trend services as well.

I wanted to show photos of our trend travels, *not* our styling and design direction for each brand. None of the trend information that I was presenting would be developed literally. Each trend would be translated appropriately for the Target brand in a way that made sense to our customers. I was confident that our design execution would be unique, trend right, and consistent with our brands . . . we weren't going to "copy" anything.

The presentation was very well received, and we

were confident that our execution would be ours, and ours alone.

Today's consumers are savvier than ever. Give them their credit, and always tell the truth. You have to move fast. Spend less time worrying about who's knocking you off and more time learning who your customer is.

Is for

OBSERVATION

Yogi Berra, one of my trend heroes, said, "You can observe a lot just by watching." Too often what we're looking for is right in front of our noses. We just think we're looking for something different. We miss the obvious. Or should I say, *dismiss* the obvious?

Georgia O'Keeffe once said, "No one sees a flower, really. It is so small. We haven't the time, and to see takes time." O'Keeffe had a unique ability to see beauty in the simplest objects. She spent years, a lifetime really, learning how to really see what was right there in front of her eyes and then capture it on canvas.

Too often we take for granted the fact that if we keep our eyes open and pay attention we won't miss anything important. But that's not always the case. In today's world we are bombarded with information overload, also known as TMI: Too Much Information. And too much data can sometimes get in the way of our seeing the reality of the situation.

The "F Test" is a classic example. Carefully read the sentence below, and count the number of Fs in the sentence. Reread it again, carefully:

FINISHED FILES ARE THE RE-
SULT OF YEARS OF SCIENTIF-
IC STUDY COMBINED WITH THE
EXPERIENCE OF MANY YEARS.

There are six Fs in the box, but only 15 percent of those who take this test find all of the Fs. If you counted fewer than six (most count three), you probably missed the Fs in the *of*s. To make a point about observation: you actually did *see* the six Fs, but you failed to count them. Since *of* is phonetically *ov,* the verbal left hemisphere, by taking the verbal clue, overrode the right "seeing" hemisphere and forced the wrong conclusion.

They were right there under your nose, but you couldn't really *see* them. By the way, children who don't know how to read see six Fs every time!

Learn to let go of your preconceptions. Practice *unlearning.* Stop looking for the answers you expect to find, and instead, identify and pay attention to the signposts and the indicators. Let them lead you to *where the minute is going.*

Is for

PASSION AND POSSIBILITIES

Trend tracking isn't about hunting for the one right answer; it's about revealing a multitude of possibilities and then finding a way to get others excited about those possibilities. You have to fight mediocrity with possibilities that inspire passion.

The American car industry's financial woes over the last few decades have been caused, fundamentally, by a lack of passion. Detroit struggled to offer products that American drivers really wanted to buy.

Somewhere along the line in this country we fell into a functional rut, with the infamous K-Car held up as a role model. It was basically a functional, boring, stripped down, boxy, unattractive (and that's being kind!) sedan that was supposed to be the perfect solution for the masses. Instead, Honda and Toyota became the best-selling cars in America because they offered drivers sexy, well-styled models with personality plus.

Detroit has finally begun to get the idea in the last few years. *Business Week* reported that in 1995 there were 910 different models of cars and light trucks sold in the United States. By 2002, the number of model options rose 44 percent, to 1,310. Talk about choices! Why the dramatic increase in possibilities in such a short amount of time?

As the design revolution took hold in the Rust Belt, carmakers finally began to realize that the road to success would need be paved with *passion,* not function. If they wanted to survive and return to profitability, carmakers would need to match the imports with some more exciting *possibilities* in car design.

The new VW Beetle turned the industry on its head. The PT Cruiser was also a surprising success, as were the new Ford Mustang, the Mini Cooper, and even the Hummer. All very different designs that inspired passion in very different kinds of consumers.

The head designer for Volkswagon summed up the lesson learned by the industry: "A car can't exist in the future if it doesn't show passion."

There's no one right answer, no one-size-fits-all trend. Be the Cheerleader of Possibilities for your

team. Encourage input and participation from everyone. Stay open to new ideas. Think about it: nothing dampens enthusiasm and passion faster than *can't*s and *never*s.

Is for

QUINTESSENCE

Unfortunately, *quintessence* isn't a word you hear too often these days. Maybe it's because store shelves are filled with too many commodities—too many bland necessities that are totally uninspiring. Quintessential products have an aura of "rightness" and authenticity that transcends trends. Think of Swiss Army knives, Mont Blanc pens, the perfect martini, or Diamond kosher salt. It's important to realize that when the world seems a little out of control, or it feels like our values have gone askew, the opposite of trendy can be very trendy.

Most people would consider rice pudding a commodity—a bland dessert that only your grandparents might have thought could be considered a quintessential treat. Not too many people today would imagine that rice pudding could be turned from a commodity into a luxurious dessert worth going out of your way for.

Rice to Riches has done just that. This small storefront in Nolita, New York's trendy neighborhood adjacent to SoHo, has given rice pudding a makeover. Customers are traveling "off the eaten path" and waiting in line for up to twenty minutes to indulge in one of their twenty-plus gourmet flavors of rice pudding.

Five dollars will buy you a bowl of "Surrender to Mango," "Coconut Coma," "Pray for Praline," or "Cinnamon Sling" (with raisins!). Their Web site brags that by combining optimum hand-picked ingredients from around the world, they offer a dessert that is so threatening they were told by the government to keep their recipes confidential!

Every design aspect of this unique dessert store is quintessential, from the flavors to the toppings, from the tables to the serving bowls. Even the front window is shaped like a grain of rice. It reminds you of a chic gelateria like you'd find in Rome or Milan . . . and the chic crowd that indulges in this quintessential treat enjoys every morsel of their just desserts.

As Betty Cornfeld and Owen Edwards note in their book *Quintessence,* "there are things . . . and then there are Things." It's easy to get caught up in the frenzy of tracking trends and to forget about the really good Things that seem to last forever. Don't be so focused on the next big thing that you forget about those Things that are always in style.

Is for

RESONATE

IN A
WORLD OF
VANILLA HOTELS
THINK OF US
AS A
Dreamsicle.

HOTEL MONACO
CHICAGO

1-800-397-7661

My dictionary says that when something is *resonant* it has an amplified effect, and that it is prolonged, sustained, vibrant. In order for a trend to resonate, it has to connect with what your audience considers important. That is to say, it must be consistent with their core values. When you consistently hit the right notes, you are on your way to striking trend chords that resonate deeply with your customer.

As a frequent traveler I've spent many a night in a hotel, some more pleasant than others. The popularity of trendy boutique hotels has greatly elevated the standard for style and luxurious amenities and raised the bar of our expectations. It used to be that if the linens were fresh, the bathroom was clean, and the property was reasonably quiet, you could expect a good night's sleep—and after all, wasn't that what you were paying for?

Not anymore. Today we expect much more than a

good night's sleep. The Hotel Monaco chain of boutique hotels doesn't disappoint. They offer a stay that
really resonates with my values, striking all the right
trend cords when it comes to extra touches and special
details that matter to me.

What's so special about Hotel Monaco? The first
time I stayed at the Monaco in Chicago I arrived late in
the evening. My flight had been delayed because of
heavy rains, I hadn't eaten, and I was feeling quite
bedraggled. I was met at the curb by a doorman with a
smile and an umbrella. He wheeled my luggage into the
lobby, right up to the front desk, where a plate of hot,
fresh-baked chocolate cookies was sitting on the coun-
tertop. The check-in manager must have read the hunger
in my eyes; he greeted me with a smile and extended the
plate to offer me one of the warm cookies. Then even I
was smiling.

I was checked in with considerable speed and handed
a key card that immediately piqued my attention. The
front of the cardholder read "Indulge Your Senses."
The plastic key card inside was imprinted with this
message: "In a world of vanilla hotels, think of us as a
Dreamsicle." Their logo is a retro-inspired drawing of
the old-fashioned bellhops and porters from the era of

luxury ocean liners. The card itself was colorful and well-designed. I couldn't wait to see what "indulgences" awaited me in my room.

I wasn't disappointed. The linens were extravagantly detailed and luxurious, with a pashmina-like shawl draped across the end of the bed. The bed pillows were numerous and voluminous. All the expected amenities were there as well: high-speed Internet connection, fax machine, hair dryer, iron and ironing board, a well-stocked mini-bar, etc. The bathroom didn't disappoint either: lots of fluffy towels, Aveda soap and hair products, and even aromatherapeutic "bath bombs" (colorfully wrapped and presented on a pewter tray) for a luxurious bathing experience.

But for me, the special touch that finished off the masterpiece was when I went to hang my clothes and found a *leopard-print*, fluffy, terry-cloth bathrobe hanging in the closet instead of the usual "vanilla" (i.e., white) robe.

After a great night's sleep filled with sweet dreams, I headed off to my appointments the next morning renewed and refreshed. I wasn't surprised to find complimentary, freshly brewed Starbucks coffee available from a server's cart in the lobby. But I was surprised to learn that in the evenings the Monaco offered complimentary wine in the whimsically decorated yet elegantly comfortable lobby. As a businesswoman traveling alone, I was much more comfortable unwinding with a glass of wine there than I would have been at a bar.

Wherever I go, my first choice in hotels is a Hotel Monaco. They really are a Dreamsicle in a world of vanilla hotels.

Whether you are designing a collection of clothes or creating the ultimate service experience, it's important to realize that each note you compose has to ring true to your audience. Even one false note can damage the overall impact of your brand.

S

Is for

SOUL

Charles Handy says, "Soul is one of those concepts that, like beauty, evaporates when you try to define it, but like beauty it is instantly recognizable when you meet it." Trends with soul have an element of energy, excitement, excellence, and desirability that connects on a special level with customers. Products with soul are easy to fall in love with, and much sought after in a marketplace awash in mediocrity.

Unfortunately, there is no formula for soul. Products with soul can be big or small, useful or frivolous, cheap or expensive, simple or fancy, elegant or exotic. You can't measure, flow chart, dictate, or expedite soul. The secret ingredient is unknown, yet it's recognized by all when it's seen.

For instance, I think the Mini Cooper and the Hummer are both vehicles with a lot of soul. They couldn't be further apart in size, price, shape, and heritage. Yet they both inspire legions of loyal customers who are passionate about their Minis or their Hummers.

I've heard of Mini Cooper owners who have formed touring clubs in their areas. I have a friend in Greenwich, Connecticut, who bought a Mini the first year they were on the market. Not long after the purchase, I spoke with her, and the conversation drifted to what our respective weekend plans were. She happily offered that she was going "touring with the Mini Cooper club." She didn't know the other owners prior to belonging to the club. It was as though the car had so much personality in its design DNA that Mini lovers just banded together spontaneously and took to the roads.

Same thing with the Hummer, except Hummer owners get together to go "off-roading" in special parks and locations that challenge the Hummer in ways that are more true to its military heritage than are regular rush-hour traffic and everyday city driving. These are serious enthusiasts. They share experiences, locations, navigational advice, and other Hummer tips in a sort of "special code."

Other products with soul include the iMac and the iPod. IPod enthusiasts are almost cultlike in their obsession with the iPod—inspiring the term *poddicts*.

Harley-Davidson motorcycles, In-and Out Burgers, OXO garlic presses, Breitling watches, and Jones Soda all have soul. In essence, they mean more than just what they are.

Can you find soul in your product or organization? If you're not sure that you'll know it when you see it, then go out of your way to hire people who will. People with soul follow their bliss. They can turn walls into doors. They are authentic, passionate, optimistic, and driven to deliver the best products and experiences possible. Their rarity makes them easy to identify.

T

Is for

TRANSLATE

There are oceans of great trends out there waiting to be discovered—tons of good ideas, loads of information, and buckets of inspiration. But not all are relevant to your customers. It's so important to translate the trends into something that's meaningful to their lives. Without that translation you might as well be speaking a foreign language. *Capice?*

These days, cell phones can do just about anything. In addition to receiving and sending calls, they can be customized with the owners' personalized ring tones. They can take pictures and send them instantly over the Internet to loved ones halfway around the world. They can send text messages, take messages, store data, speed dial, react to voice commands from the owner, etc. The trends in cell-phone functions and accessories are endless.

LG Electronics, a South Korean consumer electronics and telecom giant, wanted to find a way to deliver a trend-right cell phone to all of their customer segments. They found a unique way to translate the capabilities of modern technology specifically for the Arab world.

They developed the first *Qiblah* mobile phone, which has an indicator that points to Mecca. When the call to prayer comes, the faithful only need to pull out their cell phones, and specialized GPS technology will point the correct direction to Mecca. Some phones even store text from the Koran, and others have a special warning signal that indicates the appropriate hour to offer prayers.

Technology today can deliver an endless variety of options and functions for just about any product. Good trend research looks to find a way to effectively translate the capabilities of modern technology into a meaningful advantage for special customer segments.

It's really just another way to talk about consumer-centric design, which goes back to the age-old adage: listen to your customer. The signals are there; you just need to tune in and translate them effectively. If you do that, your customers will be singing your praises.

Avoid literal translations of any trend concept or hot idea. It's hard to differentiate yourself when you merely copy what's already out there. Think about how a

musical score translates notes and sounds into emotion. There are a limited number of notes, but musicians have been arranging them into endless versions of original music for centuries.

Is for

UNABASHED
ENTHUSIASM

Have you noticed a lack of genuine enthusiasm in corporate America these days? How many meetings have you attended recently that left you feeling really *pumped?* When was the last time you heard anyone say, with real enthusiasm, *"I LOVE it!"?* Can you remember the last time you *jumped for joy* or *squealed with delight?* If you can't get excited about your own products, just imagine how uninspired and unenthused your customers must be feeling.

In the old days (the dinosaur department-store era), buyers and fashion people were too enthusiastic about everything, seldom giving any real thought to whether the products would actually sell. Everything was "mahhh-velous, dahhhling." Who cared if it sold, as long it looked great?

Because of all of this fake enthusiasm, somewhere along the line it became gauche to show any *real* emotion when reviewing product. If you were serious about making money, you had to be serious about everything. I never really understood it. It seemed to me that creating new products and developing unique concepts to delight customers should have been the *fun* part of the job. But that didn't seem to be the case in too many product meetings that I attended in the corporate world.

I always loved bringing new, talented, and energetic designers onto my team. But I admit I often worried about the effect that too many presentations to dull-eyed, poker-faced merchants would have on their energy, their enthusiasm, and their careers.

One designer in particular stands out in my mind. Jill was a talented twentysomething industrial designer, fresh out of school. We hired her as an intern, and right from the beginning her enthusiasm was infectious. She could come up with wonderful, fresh ideas for just about anything, and would find a way to render the idea in such a manner that even the most conservative merchants would find themselves grinning.

Now, you wouldn't think that too many people could get excited about designing hardware. But buyers in the Home Improvement Department at Target needed a new concept developed for a bathroom accessory collection—you know, things like cup holders, tub accessories, bath mats, toothbrush holders, etc. At the time, we offered successful but standard-styled collections in chrome and other basic materials. The buyer was requesting something different, unique, perhaps styled specifically for children's baths.

Jill came up with a concept called "Below the Bubbles." It was a colorful, whimsical collection of tub-spout protectors, bath mats, toy holders for the tub, and toothbrush holders. Jill named the characters after sea life . . . and please note that this was long before *The Little Mermaid* or *SpongeBob SquarePants* hit the scene.

Wally the Whale was a blue tub-spout protector and Crabby the Crab was a netted toy bag that attached to the tub walls. Stan the Singing Starfish was a toothbrush holder designed to hold two toothbrushes in his rounded starfish "arms." Jill designed Stan with a special feature: a button in the center of his tummy that the child could press to make Stan sing.

I'm not exaggerating when I say that when she first presented her idea, no one thought it would fly. But Jill went to work, enthusiastically drawing sketches, making models, and developing packaging concepts in such a way that the collection would make a big splash with the little ones. When she finally did make a presentation to the buyers, she was able to coax big smiles onto their faces.

Unbeknownst to us all, she had written a song for Stan to sing that would encourage kids to brush for exactly one minute, the length of time the American Dental Association recommended. She went to a recording studio and actually recorded the song herself, imbedded the voice chip into the plastic model, and then presented the whole concept to the buying group.

Her enthusiasm was indeed contagious. The product was unique and the buyers were inspired to take a risk. Grandmothers everywhere snatched up Stan, but I don't think he would have ever made it off the drawing board and into kids' bathrooms if not for Jill's unabashed enthusiasm.

Enthusiasm, like laughter, is infectious. Go spread some around. Infect as many people as you possibly can. You'll be amazed at the change in the environment!

Is for

VORACIOUS APPETITE
FOR KNOWLEDGE

Trend trackers and creative types tend to be very curious people. We exhibit a voracious appetite for knowledge. Louis Ross, chief technology officer for Ford Motor Co., says, "In your career, knowledge is like milk. It has a shelf life stamped right on the carton." The implication is that if you're not adding to what you know on a regular basis, your career is going to turn sour, fast. In the knowledge economy, if you're not *learning* on a continual basis, chances are you won't be *earning* much either.

Books are one of the best ways we can constantly replenish our knowledge. Unfortunately, in our fast-paced world many feel that there isn't time to read all the books we'd like to. I know that was the case with my trend and design team at Target. I squeezed my reading in on long cross-country flights, and I'd bring several books along with me to read during my infrequent vacations.

Because reading has always been important to me, I try to find ways to squeeze more of it into my day. When I find a good book, I want to make the most of it. When I read Tim Sanders's book *Love is the Killer App,* it resonated deeply with me. I thought I was the only one who took notes, highlighted in the margins, and marked up her favorite books—at least until I read about Tim's passion for books, and the wisdom he believes in passing along.

I eventually developed a shorthand version of notetaking. As I read, I make notes of key words or phrases on the empty back pages and inside covers of the book. I use exclamation points, underline, highlight, circle, and even draw doodles to remind myself of the things that I find interesting or important.

As I would finish a particularly good book, I'd bring it to my staff meetings to share my learnings with my team. I'd recap the key points and share the stories that I found most interesting, and then offer to lend the book to anyone who might be interested. The books accumulated on the shelf, and so did the dust.

I discovered, though, that it wasn't necessarily for lack of interest. Often I'd be in a design meeting and hear a designer make mention of one of the facts I'd shared in the book reviews in a staff meeting. That gave me the idea to prepare short, one-page "book reports" on my favorite reads. Each was essentially a review of the key points, with some of the relevant anecdotes sprinkled in. Twice a month I'd bring in a new book, share my findings, and then hand out my book report (with key page numbers attached in case anyone wanted to delve deeper into an interesting subject).

It was a great way for me to recap what was important, put it into a format that I could easily refer back to, and share the information with my team.

Read, learn, do, explore, experience, but most of all *read*. And I mean *books*. Books give you knowledge, not just information or awareness. Ask your gurus to recommend their favorite books, and share yours with them. Spread the wisdom.

W

Is for

WALK IN OTHER WORLDS

Trendmasters are a unique species. Our innate curiosity fuels a deep desire for new experiences. We're not afraid to walk in other worlds. We often take the road less traveled. We know that unplanned, uncharted left turns will take us to the wild side. And maybe that's where we'll find *the next big thing.*

How did Americans, as a dynamic and brave nation, become so risk averse, so afraid of change? Everywhere you look there are numerous safety precautions, warnings, and mandates to do this or do that, all for our own good. Personally, I'm all for safety considerations, but I'm also in favor of a little risk-taking. There's a great saying: A ship is safe in the harbor, but that's not what it was built for.

I believe that life is meant to be an adventure, a learning, an exploration, an *experience.* We've gotten so sucked into such a virtual world that it seems we are doing less real living and more "virtual" living than ever before.

Many of us spend more time in front of some kind of screen (a computer, a TV, a video game monitor, a cell phone) than we actually do *doing* anything real. That's scary!

Life is too short and goes by too quickly not to take a few side trips along the way. Sometimes the best finds are the unexpected treats, the little wake-up calls, the anecdotes that develop from getting lost or giving up total control.

Last year I traveled to Southeast Asia to visit Angkor Wat, the ancient Khmer temple in the jungles of Cambodia. The first morning in Phnom Penh I decided to go for an early morning run. Phnom Penh was once considered the Paris of Southeast Asia; the French colonized it and built a beautiful capital city with expansive, tree-lined boulevards and beautiful parks.

Before I headed out I checked with the concierge to see if it was "safe" to go running alone. It was rush hour (lots of bikes and mopeds, very few cars) and there were lots of people about. He said yes, and suggested I take a left out of the hotel and head down to the temple in the park at the end of the avenue, and then come back by the same route.

I headed out, red Nikes and white ball cap clearly signifying to all that I was American. When I got to the end of the avenue I found myself at a traffic circle that surrounded an ancient Buddhist temple. I couldn't resist. I went up the hill, checked out the temple, came back down the hill, and headed up what I *thought* was the same street I'd run down. When I got to the end of that street, however, nothing looked remotely familiar.

I admit it. My heart was beating a little faster. I didn't know a word of Cambodian, and I hadn't brought along any cash for a pedicab, or even a key or card from the hotel with the address of where I was staying. Rather than panicking, I decided to run all the way back to the temple and walk carefully around the traffic circle, looking for something that would spark a memory and indicate which street I should take to return to my hotel.

Well, of course it wasn't that easy. I walked around the circle twice, and couldn't decide upon a course to take. As I was backing up to try to get a different perspective on the situation, I backed into something that hadn't been there a minute ago.

I turned around, looked up, and realized I had just backed right into an *elephant!* A young man was standing on top of a small, flat platform on the back of the elephant, changing a bulb in an art deco streetlamp. He saw my obvious surprise and confusion and called down "Can I help you?" In *English!* I was saved. He pointed out the avenue leading to my hotel, and I was back safely a few minutes later. Now I have to tell you, I wouldn't trade that travel experience for all the tea in Cambodia!

I can't encourage you enough to take off the blinders, get out of your ruts, be brave and daring and adventurous, even if it's only once in a while (although I believe in getting outside your box a little bit each day). Your perspective will change dramatically, and you'll have some great stories to tell in your old age!

Find the fringe! Embrace deviance! Habits are ruts. If you're reading the same magazines, shopping at the same stores, ordering the same thing from the menu of your favorite restaurant, or taking the same route to work every day, stop! Head for uncharted territory, and brace yourself for an eye-opening, off-road trend trip.

Is for

(E)XAGGERATE

We often take it for granted that everyone can easily see what we see so clearly. After all, it's right under their noses. But that's just not how it works.

Once you become a Trendmaster you tend to forget what it was like before your antennae were always up. That's why it's important to exaggerate your point, highlight the details, and magnify your message. Make sure your message can't be missed.

There are many ways to effectively make a point or present an idea. Too often, companies go to the wrong kind of extremes to try to get their message across to the consumer. Shock or schlock value may work in the short-term, but often the backlash isn't worth the negative reaction it may create. The point that you're exaggerating needs to be connected to an important value or desire of the consumer.

I heard a great story about a critical design problem

involving fighter jets during the Vietnam War that was solved in a very understated, yet exaggerated manner.

Near the end of the war, as fighting became very heavy over the Gulf of Tonkin, we began to lose way too many fighter pilots, who were not ejecting in time after their planes were shot down. They went down with their planes and died, many believed needlessly. Military officials were concerned that perhaps the ejection warning systems in the planes weren't operating effectively or properly.

They called together a team of pilots, designers, engineers, technicians, and military experts to study the situation. They determined that the red flashing light was bright enough and the warning signal to eject was loud enough, but that for some reason that went to the core of basic human instinct, the pilots remained convinced until it was *too late* that they could, indeed, save their plane if they just had another . . . second.

After much analysis, research, and thought, the solution turned out to be very simple. Instead of an obnoxious warning sound to indicate it was time to eject, they used the voice of a little girl saying "Daddy, Daddy. Eject!"

Everyone involved, especially the wives of the fighter

pilots, deemed the new "packaging" for the ejection system a success.

In a world where the choices are endless, it's critical to ensure that your customers can find what they're looking for, even if they don't know what it is. Visual presentation, signing, and packaging all play important roles in making sure the trend message gets heard. Once you have perfected your product, don't stop there. Exaggerate the obvious and carry the trend story out to the nth degree with incredible visuals, seductive signing, and clever, well-designed packaging.

Is for

YUM, YUCK, AND YAWN

Yum, yuck, and yawn are critical elements of what I call the Trend Taste Test. They are descriptions of how our *gut* feels when we are struggling with an imminent decision. It's been proven that in the realm of complexity, good decisions come from the informed gut. In other words, once you've done your trend homework and something *feels* right, that's your intuition saying *Yum— go with it!* If it doesn't *feel* right, that's a *Yuck—forget it.* And a *yawn?* If you're bored, don't you think your customers will be too?

Business today is more complicated and competitive than ever. There are decisions to be made at every turn. Most managers would say they need all the help they can get, yet they often ignore their guts in favor of the numbers. *Yum* and *Yuck* are descriptive terms for how your gut feels when you're faced with an important decision. While these terms may be hard to quantify, there is some hard-core data supporting the importance of listening to your gut.

Tom Peters tells a great story about Akio Morita, chairman and cofounder of Sony Corporation. He asked Akio how he made the decision whether or not to go into production with a new product concept. Akio told Tom that he had his designers and engineers make a presentation to him, and then he'd go home and go to sleep. If he woke up the next morning and felt good, the product was a go. If his stomach was upset when he awoke, it was a sign to him that his gut was saying "no go."

Akio's track record was pretty good. Between 1950 and 1980, Sony introduced many new products that were disruptive innovations, such as TVs, portable radios, VCRs, and the Walkman. Sony became an industry leader, and in many product categories managed to dethrone existing industry powerhouses.

Yet in the eighties, things changed dramatically. Between 1980 and 1997 Sony did not introduce a single disruptive innovation. They continued to offer improvements to their existing products, but these were mostly styling and design innovations rather than disruptive technological innovations. What happened?

In the 1980s, Akio withdrew from active management in order to become involved in Japanese politics. The company began to hire marketing and product-planning professionals who brought with them data-intensive, analytical processes for doing market research.

It turns out that those research processes were very good at uncovering unmet customer needs in markets with products that already existed, but they were bad at making the intuitive bets required to launch truly innovative ideas.

Prior to 1980 all new product launch decisions were made by Akio Morita and a small, trusted team of associates. They didn't do market research. They believed that if markets did not exist, they couldn't very well be analyzed. Their decision process was basically a Yum, Yuck, Yawn test that relied on personal intuition.

When you're faced with an important decision, why not try the Trend Taste Test? Think. Feel. Swallow. Yum? Yuck? Yawn? You know what to do next.

Z

Is for

ZEN

"When opposites supplement each other, everything is harmonious." Lao Tzu, an ancient Chinese philosopher, captured the essence of what fascinates me most about the art of trend tracking. For every yin there is a yang. For every trend there is a countertrend. In true Zen fashion, embrace opposites. Celebrate duality. Embrace polarity. *Namaste.*

Just when you think you have a trend figured out, beware! I can almost guarantee you that there is a subculture out there somewhere fanatically connected to the complete opposite of whatever it is you just deemed trendy. Sometimes it's even the same people engaging in extremely contradictory behavior. Everywhere you look there are yin-yang trends.

A few years ago, when video game sales skyrocketed, sales of old-fashioned board games took off too. As Sony racked up sales of PlayStation, Cranium became a huge hit. Retailers fought for their fair share of Play-

Station allocations just as family game nights flourished and sales of board games like Monopoly and Candy Land experienced double-digit increases.

Is the trend in cars over the last few years bigger and more in-your-face (Hummers and supersized SUVs)? Or smaller and cuter (the VW Beetle and the Mini Cooper)? Ford recently came out with a *compact hybrid SUV*: the Escape HUV. Talk about a paradox!

Fast-food restaurants proliferated just as the Slow Food movement took off. Our waistlines increased, and so did membership in health clubs across the country.

We are, according to *British Elle*, "the Ecstasy and Echinacea generation." Women who insist on eating only the best organic natural foods think nothing at all of injecting themselves with Botox (essentially a form of botulism) to help nature along a bit.

Bottom line: it's hip to contradict. So go with the flow. Don't get caught up in absolutes. Learn to be comfortable with utterly opposed trends. Paradoxes are charmingly intriguing. F. Scott Fitzgerald said, "The test of a first-class mind is the ability to hold two opposing ideas in the head at the same time and still be able to function." Learn to practice the Zen of Trend.

RECOMMENDED READING

These books are some of my all-time favorites. They have resonated deeply with me. Through the years, they fed my voracious appetite for knowledge, pushed my magic button, fused my philosophies, helped hone my instinct and intuition, filled my heart, and touched my soul. I hope you enjoy them as much as I do.

On Paradise Drive by David Brooks
Quintessence by Betty Cornfeld and Owen Edwards
The New Culture of Desire by Melinda Davis
The Lexus and the Olive Tree by Thomas L. Friedman
Purple Cow by Seth Godin
The Tao Jones Averages by Bennett W. Goodspeed
Leading the Revolution by Gary Hamel
The Age of Paradox by Charles Handy
The Elephant and the Flea by Charles Handy
The Hungry Spirit by Charles Handy
Orbiting the Giant Hairball by Gordon MacKenzie

The Road Less Traveled by M. Scott Peck, M.D.
Re-imagine! by Tom Peters
Love Is the Killer App by Tim Sanders
The Paradox of Choice by Barry Schwartz
Trading Up by Michael Silverstein and Neil Fiske
The Power of Simplicity by Jack Trout
Desert Queen by Janet Wallach
The Rise of the Creative Class by Richard Florida
The Art of Possibility by Rosamund Stone Zander and
    Benjamin Zander

ACKNOWLEDGMENTS

"In everyone's life, at some time, our inner fire goes out. It is then burst into flame by an encounter with another human being. We should all be thankful for those people who rekindle the inner spirit."
—Albert Schweitzer

With these words, I called to order my first annual personal board of directors meeting. I was forty-nine years old and I wanted to change my life. I announced my desire to leave the corporate world before I turned fifty, and shared my dream of writing a book. Thank you to the founding members and current board of directors for helping to rekindle my spirit and for fanning the flames along the way. Without your friendship, wisdom, encouragement, and support, my dreams would have gone up in smoke. Instead, they ignited!

Special thanks to Helen Chargo, my coach and friend, for helping me to understand that a dream is worth pursuing, even if you think it can never happen. And to

Elder Carson III, my friend and muse, whose incredible designs defined my original vision and continue to refine my personal brand today. Thanks also to Tom Peters, who inspired me to "go for the WOW!" throughout my entire career.

My RW Trend mantra is: "Make it Real. Keep it Simple. Make it Happen." I am forever grateful to Jonathon Lazear, my creative and inspiring agent, who helped to make this dream real, and Adrian Zackheim, my publisher, who *really* made it all real. I am grateful for the graceful editing of my talented and word-worthy editors, Will Weisser and Megan Casey. Their "E Is for Edit" expertise helped make *The Trendmaster's Guide* happen.

And if a picture is worth a thousand words, then thousands of thank yous go to Lindsay Van De Weghe for her simply witty and wonderful illustrations.

The big red bull's-eye was a great trend training ground. The lessons learned at Target were invaluable. I am grateful for the incredible opportunities and wonderful adventures that occurred along the way as Target morphed into *Tarzhay*.

Lastly, I offer my humble thanks to every designer who has ever desired to make the world a better place. Keep up the good work!

ABOUT THE AUTHOR

Robyn Waters has spent the last thirty years tracking and translating trends into sales and profits for corporate America. Most recently she was Vice President of Trend, Design, and Product Development for Target.

She is currently the president and founder of RW Trend, a trend consulting company based in Minneapolis, Minnesota. She has been described as an Ambassador of Trend, a Champion of Design, a Builder of Brands, and a Cheerleader of Possibilities. She believes that good design doesn't have to be expensive, and that everyone can appreciate good taste.

Visit her online at www.rwtrend.com.

ABOUT THE ILLUSTRATOR

Lindsay Van De Weghe is a seventeen-year-old self-taught graphic designer who lives in Minneapolis.